D0765320

NORTH AMERICAN ANIMALS

Prairie Dogs

by Megan Borgert-Spaniol

BELLWETHER MEDIA • MINNEAPOLIS, MN

Note to Librarians, Teachers, and Parents:

Blastoff! Readers are carefully developed by literacy experts and combine standards-based content with developmentally appropriate text.

Level 1 provides the most support through repetition of high-frequency words, light text, predictable sentence patterns, and strong visual support.

Level 2 offers early readers a bit more challenge through varied simple sentences, increased text load, and less repetition of high-frequency words.

Level 3 advances early-fluent readers toward fluency through increased text and concept load, less reliance on visuals, longer sentences, and more literary language.

Level 4 builds reading stamina by providing more text per page, increased use of punctuation, greater variation in sentence patterns, and increasingly challenging vocabulary.

Level 5 encourages children to move from "learning to read" to "reading to learn" by providing even more text, varied writing styles, and less familiar topics.

Whichever book is right for your reader, Blastoff! Readers are the perfect books to build confidence and encourage a love of reading that will last a lifetime!

This edition first published in 2017 by Bellwether Media, Inc.

No part of this publication may be reproduced in whole or in part without written permission of the publisher. For information regarding permission, write to Bellwether Media, Inc., Attention: Permissions Department, 5357 Penn Avenue South, Minneapolis, MN 55419.

Library of Congress Cataloging-in-Publication Data

Names: Borgert-Spaniol, Megan, 1989- author.
Title: Prairie Dogs / by Megan Borgert-Spaniol.
Other titles: Blastoff! Readers. 3, North American Animals.
Description: Minneapolis, MN : Bellwether Media, Inc., [2017] | Series: Blastoff! Readers. North American Animals | Audience: Ages 5-8. | Audience: K to grade 3. | Includes bibliographical references and index.
Identifiers: LCCN 2015046395 | ISBN 9781626174023 (hardcover : alk. paper)
Subjects: LCSH: Prairie dogs–Behavior–Juvenile literature. | Prairie dogs–Juvenile literature.
Classification: LCC QL737.R68 B66 2017 | DDC 599.36/7–dc23
LC record available at http://lccn.loc.gov/2015046395

Printed in the United States of America, North Mankato, MN.

Table of Contents

What Are Prairie Dogs?

Prairie dogs are **rodents** with short legs and thick bodies.

In the Wild

N
W   E
S

Extinct

Extinct in the Wild

Critically Endangered

Endangered

Vulnerable

Near Threatened

Least Concern

prairie dog range = ▢

conservation status: least concern
(endangered in some regions)

They are found in the flat, open grasslands of central and western North America.

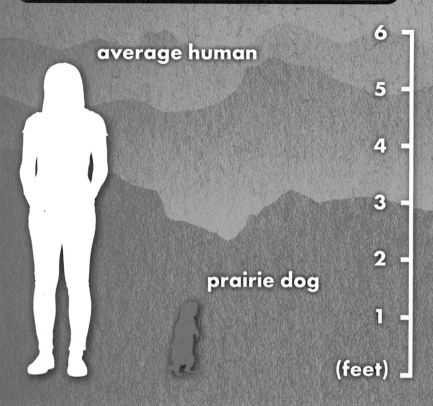

Size of a Prairie Dog

average human

prairie dog

6
5
4
3
2
1
(feet)

Prairie dogs are usually 12 to 15 inches (30 to 38 centimeters) long.

Their strong legs and long nails help them dig **burrows**. These underground tunnels can be miles long!

Finding Food

Prairie dogs **forage** outside their burrows during the day. These **herbivores** feed on grasses and other plants.

western wheatgrass

blue grama grass

sand dropseed

sun sedge

plains pricklypear

scarlet globemallow

They do not have to drink much water. They get it from the food they eat!

Food is harder to find in fall and winter. Some prairie dogs **hibernate** during this time.

Others stay in their burrows for several days in a row.

In spring, females give birth inside their burrows. They feed and **groom** their **pups**. Pups leave the burrow after about six weeks. They forage and play together outside.

Baby Facts

Name for babies:	pups
Size of litter:	3 to 4 pups
Length of pregnancy:	about 1 month
Time spent with mom:	about 1 year

Coteries and Colonies

Prairie dogs live in small groups called **coteries**. A coterie usually includes a male, several females, and their young.

Identify a Prairie Dog

small ears   light brown fur   short legs

Coterie members find food and build burrows together. They also protect their **territory**.

Many coteries in the same area make up a town or **colony**. There can be hundreds of prairie dogs in one colony!

burrow
mound

A colony's land is
dotted with many
burrow **mounds**.

Colony members work together to stay safe from **predators**. Prairie dogs called **sentries** keep watch on top of their burrow mounds.

coyotes

bobcats

American badgers

black-footed ferrets

prairie rattlesnakes

golden eagles

They bark to warn others when danger is near. Then the prairie dogs have time to escape to their burrows.

The guards use different calls
for different predators.

They also have an all-clear call. This tells the colony it is safe to come out!

Glossary

burrows—holes or tunnels that some animals dig for homes

colony—a group of prairie dogs; a prairie dog colony is a town of many coteries.

coteries—families of prairie dogs that live together

forage—to go out in search of food

groom—to clean or make neat

herbivores—animals that only eat plants

hibernate—to spend the winter sleeping or resting

mounds—piles of dirt; prairie dogs make mounds around the entrances of burrows.

predators—animals that hunt other animals for food

pups—baby prairie dogs

rodents—small animals that gnaw on their food

sentries—guards of entrances; prairie dog sentries warn others of danger.

territory—the land area where an animal lives

To Learn More

AT THE LIBRARY

Aronin, Miriam. *The Prairie Dog's Town: A Perfect Hideaway.* New York, N.Y.: Bearport Pub., 2010.

George, Lynn. *Prairie Dogs: Tunnel Diggers.* New York, N.Y.: PowerKids Press, 2011.

Zuchora-Walske, Christine. *Let's Look at Prairie Dogs.* Minneapolis, Minn.: Lerner Publications Co., 2010.

ON THE WEB

Learning more about prairie dogs is as easy as 1, 2, 3.

1. Go to www.factsurfer.com.

2. Enter "prairie dogs" into the search box.

3. Click the "Surf" button and you will see a list of related web sites.

With factsurfer.com, finding more information is just a click away.

Index

The images in this book are reproduced through the courtesy of: Henk Bentlage, front cover; MyImages - Micha, pp. 4, 15 (top left); Eric Isselee, pp. 6, 15 (bottom); mubus7, p. 7; Steffen Wchter/ Glow Images, p. 8; Sheri Hagwood/ USDA, p. 9 (top left); Bildagentur Zoonar GmbH, p. 9 (top right); Matt Lavin/ Wikipedia, p. 9 (center left, center right); Binh Thanh Bui, p. 9 (bottom left); Tom Willard, p. 9 (bottom right); SuperStock/ Glow Images, p. 10; Anna Biller, p. 11; Mikael Males, p. 12; All-stock-photos, p. 13; S.Cooper Digital, p. 14; RONORMANJR, p. 15 (top center); TOMO, p. 15 (top right); Elle1, p. 16; Tom & Pat Leeson/ a/ Age Fotostock, p. 17; aabeele, p. 18; Cynthia Kidwell, p. 19 (top left); Svetlana Foote, p. 19 (top right); pschoenfelder, p. 19 (center left); USFWS Mountain Prairie/ Wikipedia, p. 19 (center right); taviphoto, p. 19 (bottom left); withGod, p. 19 (bottom right); Max Allen/ Alamy, p. 20; Don Johnston/ Glow Images, p. 21.